T0362586

MONEY TALKS

Capitalist ethics, colonialism

and divine governance

No slave can serve two masters; for a slave will either hate
the one and love the other or be devoted to the one
and despise the other. You cannot serve God and wealth.
Luke 16:13

Other Books published by Coventry Press by or about John Bottomley

At Work with John's Gospel
A Spirituality for Life's Fruitfulness in all our Labours
Five Bible Studies

The Struggle for Justice
Conversations with John Bottomley about Transforming Church
Community Services
(Kate Dempsey)

**Bible Studies
in search of Christ's Healing,
Justice & Reconciliation**

A University of Divinity
Religion & Social Policy Network
Engagement Project

Money
Talks

Capitalist Ethics,
Colonialism & Divine Governance

John Bottomley

COVENTRY
PRESS

Published in Australia by
Coventry Press
33 Scoresby Road
Bayswater VIC 3153

ISBN 9781922589156

Catalogue-in-Publication entry is available from the National Library of
Australia http://catalogue.nla.gov.au

Cover design by Ian James – www.jgd.com.au
Text design by Coventry Press
Set in Fontin

Printed in Australia

Contents

Acknowledgments

The Commonwealth Government's *Excellence in Research Australia 2018* policy framework mandated the need for academic research to include the evaluation of research according to its engagement with the 'non-academic world' and its impact on that world. This Bible study brings critical findings of two reports from the Religion and Social Policy Network's research with the Finance Sector Union (FSU). The FSU provided vital access to a small group of their members for our initial pilot project, and then gave RASP access to a significant data set of 353 members' comments on their experience of toxic work environments submitted to the union for the Royal Commission into Misconduct in the Banking, Superannuation and Financial Services Industry. Our liaison with Clive Pattison, FSU National Researcher Officer was pivotal to the success of this cooperative endeavour.

The support of RASP founding Director, Revd Dr Gordon Preece was important to the success of the relationship with FSU and the initiation of our research program, as was the participation of Revd Prof. John Flett and Revd Brendan Byrne to the completion of the two pieces of research.

I was grateful for the direction of Revd Dr Robyn Whitaker, Senior Lecturer in New Testament at the University of Divinity's Pilgrim Theological College, for her advice on a good commentary on Luke's Gospel and associated reading material.

Revd Dr Garry Worete Deverell, inaugural Vice Chancellor's Fellow in Indigenous Theologies at the University of Divinity, provided valuable feedback on a first draft of the studies, and offered supportive and generous encouragement for the project.

My colleague Revd Dr Richard Wilson has also provided critical comment on drafts of the studies as well as guidance for the engagement focus of this material.

John Bottomley
Religion and Social Policy Network
University of Divinity
2021

Foreword

The phrase 'money talks' usually refers to the persuasive power of money to get things done. For many workers in Australia today, too often what money gets done is the cause of harm and injustice. In 2019, more than 25 Australian businesses were forced to admit underpayment of staff; in some cases, underpayment of staff has gone on for more than a decade. The totals included amounts of $32 million, $25 million, $15 million and, for one corporation, $300 million. And it is not just workers who suffer when money talks in such harmful ways. In the banking sector, the 2018 Royal Commission uncovered that total costs relating to misconduct causing harm to customers is now more than $10 billion.

Australian churches need to be talking about money as a central part of their mission to pursue justice. In the context of Scripture, churches need to talk about how biblical testimony speaks to the just and unjust uses of money in our society today.

This has been a priority for the Religion and Social Policy Network (RASP) at the University of Divinity over the past four years. This has included a partnership with the Finance Sector Union (FSU) to produce two pieces of ground-breaking research.

A good deal of RASP's partnership with the FSU has been coordinated by the author of this study, Revd John Bottomley. For over thirty years, his fruitful ministry activities have included the support of long-term injured workers and of families bereaved by a work-related death. Now, in *Money Talks: capitalist ethics, colonialism and divine governance*, John has drawn together two of the University's most urgent priorities.

After a century of theological education and research, the University of Divinity is at last beginning to provide substantial support to recognition and growth of Aboriginal and Torres Strait Islander theologies and theologians. *Money Talks* addresses the theme of truth-telling that is so vital to the work taking place towards treaty. This study asks non-Indigenous readers to reckon with how Australia's current economic system and the business world are built on the injustice of colonial invasion. It suggests some practical ways we can contribute to the pursuit of justice.

Secondly, the University's vision is to address the issues of the contemporary world by drawing on the wisdom of ancient traditions. In *Money Talks*, we have a great source of wisdom in the concluding prayers from Psalms in each study, plus the four selections from Luke's Gospel and the concluding meditation from the Gospel of John. The final study – on the scourge of suicide in the world of work and Indigenous communities – is, for example, particularly valuable in sharpening our attention to the challenges to life and livelihood we all face, both locally and nationally, as we search for truth and fulfilment.

I trust you will find these studies engaging for you and those who undertake them with you. They are not designed to be led by an expert but are written so that the entire study group may share in reading and listening to the material provided. The emphasis on each person bringing their imagination to the task of listening and contributing draws on the strength of this way of being so evocatively lived out in Ignatian spirituality. When Christians come together to talk about money, we are called to bring our hearts and minds, bodies and souls to the conversation. I pray that you are able to enter into these studies in ways that celebrate and draw upon the lived experience of each person present.

Professor Peter Sherlock
Vice-Chancellor, University of Divinity
Melbourne
December 2021

Introduction

Talking about money is perhaps the last social taboo for Australians. We find money difficult to talk about. So, this study aims to help us talk about money because the secrecy around the use and abuse of money is the source of profound harm in Australian society. The litany of harm begins with the colonial invasion of Indigenous country in 1788, and the violent assault on Indigenous people's custodianship of country in the name of economic growth and the accumulation of wealth for the few. The national silence surrounding this injustice hides the source of the harm experienced by First Nations people to the present, due to the legacy of colonialism's idolatry of money.

The recent 2018 *Interim Report of the Royal Commission into Misconduct in the Banking, Superannuation and Financial Services Industry* found widespread and serious harm to customers of today's Australia's financial services industry. The harm identified by Commissioner Hayne has a grimly familiar ring for an economic system founded on injustice. 'Too often, the answer seems to be greed – the pursuit of short-term profit at the expense of basic standards of honesty' (Hayne, xvii). However, when you engage with the studies in this book, you may conclude that the Royal Commission pulled its punches, by failing to fully listen to the harm caused by the idolatrous nature of money in Australian society. The Royal Commission did not see the misconduct of financial services corporations in terms of their absolute love of accumulating money, putting its trust in the law to regulate the behaviour of those addicted to making money with little or no regard for God or neighbour. Lawyer and former Justice of the High Court of Australia, Kenneth Hayne AC QC, concluded 'The law sets the bounds of permissible behaviour' (Hayne, 269). Luke's Gospel advocates a different belief.

Anglican theologian Lesslie Newbigin explained what the idolatrous nature of money means for our society. It is 'the putting of something that is not God in the place belonging to God' (Newbigin, 109). This 'something' at the heart of western culture that is not God is a belief in the virtue of maximising profit, a belief about the value of money that elevates economic growth and financial success to god-like measures of personal and corporate worth. In these studies, you will be asked to listen to how this belief diminishes the God-given dignity of human life. Together, we will uncover a demonic spirituality in the ethics of maximising profit that is engaged in a deadly struggle against the governance of God's reign embodied in the life, death and resurrection of Jesus Christ.

The study gives voice to biblical wisdom, Indigenous spirituality, and those harmed by their work within the financial services industry to expose the folly of trusting the law to set the bounds of 'permissible behaviour'. These are critical voices from ancient and contemporary experiences from those who have for too long been kept silent about the harmful demonic of the idolatry of money.

These five studies have three aims:

1. To better understand how the path to national reconciliation between Indigenous and non-Indigenous Australians must account for colonialism's national idolatry of economic growth and economic progress and the harm caused by this idolatry to individual and collective life and wellbeing.
2. To empower study participants with the exercise of their agency in ensuring greater faithfulness in the use of their investments by Australian financial services institutions.
3. To give a voice to those silenced by Australia's idolatrous reverence of our economy. In this study, you will hear three voices to enrich your understanding of the need for justice ethics in economic life.

   i. The Word of God speaks to you through the Gospels and the wisdom of Indigenous spirituality. Four studies will listen to texts from Luke's Gospel and the fifth focuses on a reading from John's Gospel. While these five texts are from year C of the Lenten Gospel readings from the *Revised Common Lectionary*, they may be studied any time you want to connect with a solid biblical foundation for engaging modern economic issues. The Uluru 'Statement from the heart' and the encouragement and support of the Revd Dr Garry Worete Deverell, Vice Chancellor's Fellow in Indigenous Theologies, inform a perspective on Indigenous spirituality.

   ii. You will hear the voices of workers in the finance sector taken from two research reports of the University of Divinity's Religion and Social Policy Network for Australia's Finance Sector Union (FSU). Each study contains direct quotes from these workers that highlight ethical challenges they face. There is also material from academics and professionals who are working to transform the ethical environment in the Australian financial sector.

iii. We have designed the study to support study group participants to listen to one another talk about money, God and faith. Church members are also ordinary Australian customers and deposit holders or investors in the Australian finance industry, yet perhaps we have too readily acquiesced in the taboo about not speaking about money. Your voice with others across the Australian church community may bring a significant contribution to establishing fairness/justice at the boundary of financial entities permissible behaviour.

Guidelines for participants

These studies are designed so that leadership may be shared within the study group. The leader for each study should read over the study well before the session. Some people may not be used to the generous amount of time for silent reflection and meditation given in this study. Encourage them to develop a patient and open attitude to this time of listening for God's voice.

Group members' participation may be encouraged by members taking it in turn to read a paragraph at a time to engage with the material. The leader for the session can then focus on the questions and judging the time for reflection, sharing, and discussion. Plan for at least 90 minutes for each study.

For studies two and three, participants will need a pen and paper to write on. At the conclusion of study two, arrange for several group members to research the practical actions for truth-telling at the end of the study book, and prepare a summary they can report to the group during study three. For study four, you will need a white-board or butchers paper and marker pens for the 'brainstorming' activity. With brainstorming, one person writes every suggestion from the group on the board, without comment or interruption from anyone. The aim is to encourage the creative flow of thoughts, and to be aware of what triggers group members thinking.

At the end of study five, the leader of the session will be ready to note the comments from the group members you would like to feedback to the Religion and Social Policy Network.

STUDY ONE

Vocational ethics of justice and liberation

Background

Luke's Gospel is well suited for this study of money, the economy and financial services. It warns that coveting wealth is counter to God's intention for our relationships with God and neighbour (Luke 12:22-34, 16:13, 17:26-30), and it encourages generous sharing with those in need. Perhaps more than money, Jesus' followers are urged to offer a generous welcome into their community for the poor and marginalised. Such open-heartedness comes from their trust in Christ's generous provision of food and healing. True worship of God entails a 'legitimate and life-giving role for economic resources' (Carroll, p. 375) to help sustain the lives of those who lack the necessities of life, and in doing so, serves God's purposes in our world.

Jesus' message is counter-cultural for the dominant Roman society. While his message would be welcomed by those made poor by the heavy burden of Roman taxation, it also called the wealthy to cross the boundaries of status and wealth – the markers of success in the hierarchical structure of Greco-Roman society – to be in solidarity with the poor and marginalised. Yet this is not 'charity' that further honours the status of the rich and diminishes the honour and status of the poor. Luke's vision of solidarity demonstrates how both the wealthy and the poor are transformed by their alignment with a gospel founded in justice and righteousness.

The opening three chapters of Luke's Gospel sound a breath-taking fanfare for Jesus' appearance on the scene of Israel's long-awaited liberation from centuries of oppression. In these chapters, Luke presents a series of characters who look forward to God's initiative of social upheaval that will reverse the social status of rich and poor in an unjust order and will foreshadow Israel's divine deliverance from their oppression. Jesus is baptised for this task with the power of the Holy Spirit, a power conferred upon Jesus as the Son of God.

So, the stage is set. But how will Jesus carry out this historic vocation? And what does Jesus' vocation mean for our own just and wise living and for the appropriate use of our economic resources?

Luke 4:1-13

Three readers are needed to read this passage: Luke (the narrator), the devil and Jesus.

Narrator: Jesus, full of the Holy Spirit, returned from the Jordan and was led by the Spirit into the wilderness, where for forty days he was tempted by the devil. He ate nothing at all during those days, and when they were over, he was famished. The devil said to him,

Devil: If you are the Son of God, command this stone to become a loaf of bread.

Narrator: Jesus answered him,

Jesus: It is written, 'One does not live by bread alone'.

Narrator: Then the devil led him up and showed him in an instant all the kingdoms of the world. And the devil said to him,

Devil: To you I will give their glory and all this authority; for it has been given over to me, and I give it to anyone I please. If you, then, will worship me, it will all be yours.

Narrator: Jesus answered him,

Jesus: It is written, 'Worship the Lord your God, and serve only him'.

Narrator: Then the devil took him to Jerusalem, and placed him on the pinnacle of the temple, saying to him,

Devil: If you are the Son of God, throw yourself down from here, for it is written, 'He will command his angels concerning you, to protect you', and 'On their hands they will bear you up, so that you will not dash your foot against a stone'.

Narrator: Jesus answered him,

Jesus: It is said, 'Do not put the Lord your God to the test'.

Narrator: When the devil had finished every test, he departed from him until an opportune time.

Formation in the ethics of God's justice

Well before Jesus encounters the devil, he has been formed by the Holy Spirit. His formation in the Spirit began at his conception (Luke 1:35) and again he was filled by the Holy Spirit at his baptism (Luke 3:22). His upbringing was marked by a mother who looked forward to God's initiative to reverse Israel's fortunes through Jesus' birth (Luke 1:46-55). Later, poor shepherds welcomed his birth, the first to receive the good news Jesus was God's liberating Messiah and Lord, and in opposition to the Roman Emperor's claim to the title of Lord (2:8-11). Jesus' upbringing formed his character in faithfulness to Jewish Law (2:22-24, 2:39-40, 2:41-51), and so he grew 'in wisdom, in stature, and in favour with God and human beings' (2:52).

How does this account of Jesus' formation and testing relate to your experience of the beliefs and ethics of modern-day workers? In a pilot study, RASP researchers asked eight FSU members what personal ethics they brought to their work in the finance industry. They said:

a. Treat people fairly and with respect: e.g. I hold strong to being treated fairly. Have respect for others in your team. Be fair to clients, to do the right thing.
b. Be honest: e.g. Be honest and trustworthy. Be honest and not mislead, correct clients when they have an incorrect understanding of the outcome or the product.
c. Be true to myself: e.g. I need to be able to sleep at night and refuse to blindly trust procedures that I don't understand or don't think are in the customer's best

interests. My ethics are derived from my upbringing and generally my workplace can't dictate what I believe.

d. Put the customer's needs first: e.g. I want to do the right thing, but often the right thing is against policy and procedure, and I feel concerned about risking my job to do it. Focus on what the customer wants and needs and don't care about company targets.

e. Don't harm others: e.g. Ensure my actions don't affect others negatively where possible.

f. Stand up against unethical practices: e.g. Call out poor, unethical or sub-standard practices, and trying to correct them.

Now reflect for a time, in silence, on any occasion when you were faced with a devilishly difficult decision at work, or elsewhere, where your decision may have an impact on others' wellbeing.

Share your reflections in turn, without interruption and listening closely to one another.

Then discuss:

- What factors in Jesus' formation as described by Luke, or from the formation of the workers' ethics listed above, are important to you and others in the study group?
- What other factors in Jesus' formation as described by Luke, or from the formation of the workers' ethics listed above, would you have liked to have at the time of your difficult decision?

Testing the integrity of God's justice ethic for human flourishing

The devil craftily probes what Jesus believes his personal ethical formation means for his future work as Israel's saviour, for the devil well understands the hopes and dreams of Jews for God's messiah. They are waiting for a messiah to rescue them from the pain and powerlessness of living under oppressive Roman rule. So, the devil addresses Jesus three times with the conditional 'if': twice saying 'if you are the Son of God', and once, 'if you bow down before me'. How could a real Son of God not want God's suffering and oppressed people to have:

1. All the bread they want, and never be hungry?
2. The power to be free of the hated Roman empire?
3. A leader who is so in lockstep with God that nothing could ever upset their plans?

What is at stake here is whether Jesus needs to side with the devil to ensure God *meets peoples' expectations* for God's messiah, or whether Jesus' relationship with God is founded on Jesus' fidelity to, and *trust in God's plans* for Israel's liberation. The devil wants to take over from God (and God's justice and righteousness) and be at the centre of authority and purpose for what happens in the world, and thus to be worshipped and adored. But with each test, Jesus reaffirms that his formation in God's justice and righteousness is at the heart of his self-understanding. Jesus will trust in God's provision, the power of God's love, and acceptance of his personal human limits to fulfil his messianic vocation to establish God's reign of justice on earth

Luke's account of Jesus' testing appears congruent with today's ethical challenges for many workers. FSU asked their members to contribute to the union's input to the Banking Royal Commission by describing the factors that made their work environment in the finance industry toxic. They described three attacks on their personal ethics.

1. *'You can have all you want'*: e.g. Some Financial Advisors are more concerned about their targets and bonuses than what was in their clients' interests. Financial Advisor

bonuses were ... rewarded on a scale of best return to the bank, not necessarily to customers.

2. *'With power comes status'*: e.g. Management applied a great deal of pressure to staff at all levels to achieve sales targets. 'Incentive' programs were implemented to encourage and reward staff. Staff are applauded for sales even though it can be detrimental to a customers' long-term needs. Those who pushed for loan approvals, even though it was evident customers could not afford the loan, received promotions and bonuses.

3. *'With your brains, what could go wrong?'* It is common practice for Branch Managers to achieve their business results by sourcing fake business. This occurs in a variety of ways, including stealing business from different branches, churning the same business repeatedly, or even asking for 'revenue' that they did not work for, solely for the purpose of inflating their business results. The wrong products are being sold to customers solely for the bank's benefit to better achieve their inflated Key Performance Indicators, meaning that there are many unsuspecting customers with inappropriate financial products due to receiving misleading advice.

Reflect for a time in silence on an occasion when you were tested at work, or elsewhere, to make a decision that violated or offended your personal ethics and integrity.

Share your reflections in turn, without interruption and listening closely to one another.

Then discuss:

- What insight does Luke's account of Jesus' testing, and the struggle of these finance sector workers bring to your understanding of this challenging or testing time in your work or elsewhere in your life?
- What resources does Luke's account of Jesus' testing, and the struggles of these finance sector workers suggest to you about resources you would value to help you face future testing times at work or elsewhere in your life?

Luke's hard-edged realism

This is only the beginning! While Luke concludes his account of Jesus' testing with a clear sense that Jesus has a deep and abiding confidence in his messianic vocation, we are reminded that the devil (usually referred to in Luke as Satan) will continue to look for weaknesses in Jesus' ministry to derail God's plans and intentions. As we will see in future studies, the focus for the forces of sin and evil will fall on Jesus' closest followers.

These forces also fall on us as we seek to understand our vocation as followers of Jesus Christ. In the financial services industry, we have witnessed how demonic forces have shaped that industry to displace God's justice at the centre of economic life. To what extent are our own life and work shaped today by similar forces of sin and evil, where God's plan to restore justice in our hearts and in our lives is now in a struggle with the greed and covetousness of modern-day capitalist ethics?

Many Christians would scoff at the idea that capitalism has any ethics. But Jiwei Ci has argued that in capitalist societies there are many ethical or moral beliefs. Some ethics have their source in the market, while others, such as religious ethics, have their source in traditions that predate capitalism. Non-market sourced ethics may exist in tension with market ethics or, alternatively, be accommodated to and fit-in with market ethics. Capitalist ethics and those non-market ethics that fit in with market ethics both help the market to maximise businesses profit-making.

Ci argues that because profit-making is a key feature of capitalism, it follows that *the profit motive must be an ethically (as opposed to merely legally) permissible motive* in society. 'The ethical permissibility of the profit motive is an extremely important fact about the ethics of capitalism' (Ci, 412). Because profit maximisation has been made a condition of survival in the market, capitalism has given profit a powerful and indispensable legitimacy. Capitalist ethics ensure there is no moral reason to shy away from legally permissible profit-making.

Ci then makes a distinction between an internal and an external way for an ethic to be related to the market. Christian social ethics seek to offer *an external ethical judgment* on the market, whereas *an ethic internally related* to the market *will never* override the profit motive. An internally related ethic of justice serves to 'temper' justice by justifying the removal of all constraints on the means of profit maximisation except those behaviours that clearly break the law. Justice is then 'tempered' by the ethical virtue of enlightened self-interest, which finds virtue in ensuring success on the market's terms: maximised profit.

- Together, draw up a list of all the businesses and industries that you believe temper justice to ensure they continue to maximise their profit.
- For each entity on your list, note the ethical virtues that individual members of your group believe have been violated or offended against. Summarise your group's findings: what aspects of God's justice and righteousness revealed in Jesus' test have been tempered?
- Discuss what may be needed to restore God's justice and righteousness to these businesses and industries.

Concluding prayer

Psalm 91:1-2, 9-16

Readers: Leader (L), people (P), right side of the group (Right), left side (Left), All.

L: You who live in the shelter of the Most High, who abide in the shadow of the Almighty, will say to the Lord,
P: 'My refuge and my fortress; my God, in whom I trust.'
L: Because you have made the Lord your refuge, the Most High your dwelling place,
P: no evil shall befall you, no scourge come near your tent.
L: For he will command his angels concerning you to guard you in all your ways.
P: On their hands they will bear you up, so that you will not dash your foot against a stone.
L: You will tread on the lion and the adder, the young lion and the serpent you will trample under foot.
P: Those who love me, I will deliver;

Right: I will protect those who know my name.
Left: When they call to me, I will answer them;
Right: I will be with them in trouble,
All: I will rescue them and honour them.
With long life I will satisfy them, and show them my salvation.

STUDY TWO

A whistle blower's destiny

Background

Jesus' journey – as told in Luke's Gospel – is marked by his acts of gracious forgiveness that restore suffering and marginalised people to the community, while still pursuing claims for divine justice. Jesus' ministry of liberating healing continues to challenge the dark forces of people's oppression, so of course those with power who owe allegiance to Satan's dominion will take every opportunity to push back. His teachings remind his followers that his assault on evil forces powerfully aligns with the promised reign of God and is unsettling to those who are benefiting from the established order.

Luke 13:31-35

Four readers are needed to read this passage: Luke (the narrator), two Pharisees and Jesus.

Narrator: At that very hour some Pharisees came and said to him,

Pharisee1: Get away from here,

Pharisee2: for Herod wants to kill you.

Narrator: He said to them,

Jesus: Go and tell that fox for me, 'Listen, I am casting out demons and performing cures today and tomorrow, and on the third day I finish my work. Yet today, tomorrow, and the next day I must be on my way, because it is impossible for a prophet to be killed outside of Jerusalem'. Jerusalem, Jerusalem, the city that kills the prophets and stones those who are sent to it! How often have I desired to gather your children together as a hen gathers her brood under her wings, and you were not willing! See, your house is left to you. And I tell you, you will not see me until the time comes when you say, 'Blessed is the one who comes in the name of the Lord'.

Calling out corrupt governance

What is 'that very hour' when the Pharisees arrive with their warning about Herod Antipas, ruler of Galilee as a client or puppet of the Roman Empire? Luke uses this phrase to link what is coming next with what has just gone before. What has just happened is that Jesus had said, 'Indeed, some are last who will be first, and some are first who will be last' (12:30). Jesus had announced the sort of reversal Mary had sung of earlier (Luke 1:51-53). We should hear that this sort of reversal is now being applied to corrupt rulers. Herod would not want to hear that God's coming reign will reverse the positions of those with wealth and power and give advantage to the poor and powerless. So, do these Pharisees know Herod is out to harm Jesus and so are trying to warn him of danger, or are they cuddling up to Herod as part of a clever ruse to scare Jesus away? Given the way Herod executed John the Baptist, Luke's audience would have no doubt either way that Herod's attitude towards Jesus carried an implied threat meant to silence Jesus.

Pause for a moment to recall when you have been silenced because you feared another person had the power to harm you.

Now consider the experience of the following FSU members who used their contributions to the Union's research for Australia's Banking Royal Commission to break their silence about the urgent need to warn others of the injustices that some finance sector managers were perpetrating on staff and customers.

▷ I became a whistle blower to expose a home loans fraud scheme, which led to the expulsion of two staff including the manager of the branch. I didn't receive any support or counselling and the matter was swept under the carpet. Eventually the bank offered me a redundancy package to remove me.

▷ We have a whistle blower protection policy... how is it staff are too scared of the repercussions to use it?

▷ I was compelled to report a multimillion-dollar case to our whistle blowing department, who were to keep everything confidential. Within days, word had spread within the business sales team. The manager approached me and asked what was going on. I had reported this in confidence and expected it was to remain private. I lost faith in the anonymous whistle blowing process and knew then privacy was a luxury in that company. It wasn't long before I was targeted.

Reflect for a time in silence on how these workers are feeling after standing up for justice at their workplace.

Then share your response, and any times you have experienced similar feelings in your work and other aspects of life.

Next, discuss what is common in the situation of Jesus, the union whistle blowers, and your own experience standing up for justice in:

- The power to speak for justice.
- The personal risk

Lamenting the harm of corrupt governance

Yet Jesus regards the real threat as not the puppet Herod, but the coalition of political and religious forces seated at

Jerusalem. So Jesus dismisses the threat of John's murderer, Herod, with the apt metaphor of 'fox', perhaps alluding to the danger of a fox in the henhouse by expressing his desire to keep Jerusalem's children safe as a hen gathers her brood under her wings. Jesus embraces this female image to express his profound compassion and sorrow for the people of a city with a reputation for killing and rejecting prophets sent by God to lead them in the ways of justice and righteousness. Jesus' anguished lament comes from his prescient awareness of the fate that awaits him at the hands of self-serving governance, and perhaps in his sorrow that such evil is a betrayal of the city's vocation to be the heart of Israel's glorifying of God. The blessing that would honour the city of God's temple takes on a bitter taste: it has lost its way.

Two bank staff who took on the role of public whistle blowers both lost their jobs with their bank but are credited with major contributions to the public demand for a Royal Commission into their industry. The journalist, Adele Ferguson, tells of an occasion during the Royal Commission when a group of ten bank victims were telling their stories over a meal with a prominent whistle blower. 'Some of these people had been fighting the banks for years. Some had been suicidal, others had suffered divorce, lost their businesses or their homes. These were the human faces of bad banking. They were the collateral damage of a system that had allowed banks to bully customers in the shadows' (Ferguson, 309). Yet when the Royal Commission had completed its enquiry in 2018, it had not called for evidence from any whistle blowers in the finance industry and had failed to make any recommendations for whistle blower protection.

Imagine how Jesus would be looking at the victims of injustice in Australia's financial services industry, and how he might feel about the legal system that failed to protect them.

What image would you use to express Jesus' sorrow and compassion for them?

After a period of silent reflection on the image that expresses Jesus' sorrow and compassion, write a brief lament that sums up Jesus' compassion and sorrow for victims of unjust banking and self-serving governance. Such a lament may include the following:

- Jesus address to God and how Jesus is feeling about what he is seeing.
- State the problem Jesus is asking God to help with.
- Express Jesus' trust in God to put things right.
- State what Jesus wants God to do.
- What does Jesus remember that gives him confidence God will bring justice to this situation?

When all have written Jesus' imagined lament, participants are invited to pray them in turn.

Closing prayer

Psalm 27

Readers: Leader (L), People (P), first voice (V1), second voice (V2), All.

L: The Lord is my light and my salvation; whom shall I fear?
P: The Lord is the stronghold of my life; of whom shall I be afraid?
L: When evildoers assail me to devour my flesh – my adversaries and foes – they shall stumble and fall.
P: Though an army encamp against me, my heart shall not fear;
though war rise up against me, yet I will be confident.
L: One thing I asked of the Lord, that will I seek after:
V1: to live in the house of the Lord all the days of my life,
V2: to behold the beauty of the Lord,
V1: and to inquire in his temple.
L: For he will hide me in his shelter in the day of trouble;
V1: he will conceal me under the cover of his tent;
V2: he will set me high on a rock.
All: Now my head is lifted up above my enemies all around me, and I will offer in his tent sacrifices with shouts of joy; I will sing and make melody to the Lord.

V1: Hear, O Lord, when I cry aloud,
V2: be gracious to me and answer me!
L: 'Come', my heart says, 'seek his face!'
V1: Your face, Lord, do I seek.
V2: Do not hide your face from me.

V1: Do not turn your servant away in anger, you who have been my help.

V2: Do not cast me off, do not forsake me, O God of my salvation!

L: If my father and mother forsake me, the Lord will take me up.

P: Teach me your way, O Lord,

and lead me on a level path because of my enemies.

V2: Do not give me up to the will of my adversaries,

V1: for false witnesses have risen against me,

V2: and they are breathing out violence.

All: I believe that I shall see the goodness of the Lord in the land of the living.

Wait for the Lord; be strong, and let your heart take courage; wait for the Lord!

STUDY THREE

It's time for national reconciliation – you are on your last chance

Background

Jesus has been teaching that the new reign of God's justice is close at hand. Are you ready? There is no excuse for not providing faithful, wise, and vigilant preparation for stepping into God's now-arriving, new era of justice for all.

But there is also a warning. God's promised justice and peace will arouse division within communities and households because many will be unwilling to disengage from their current security to grasp the liberating life that Jesus is offering. Jesus has a sharp warning to a crowd that seems to be unable to read and respond to the signs of the times. He mocks the crowd for being able to read the signs of the weather changing yet failing to grasp how decisive is this moment in history.

Perhaps Jesus' warning loses its sting for urbanised Australians, who have allowed the impacts of colonialism to blind our capacity to observe and read the changes in the weather, let alone changes in nature more broadly. But Jesus' warning may now have even more force for settler people as the cumulative crises in nature – the global COVID-19 pandemic, climate change, environmental degradation, and the rampant violation of the earth's ecology – all lead to the same pressing question: how do we evaluate 'this moment' and frame a fitting action program? (Luke 12:56).

Jesus' warning insists we will be held accountable to the future.

Luke 13:1-9

Four readers are needed to read this passage: Luke (the narrator), Jesus, the landowner and the gardener.

Narrator: At that very time there were some present who told him about the Galileans whose blood Pilate had mingled with their sacrifices. He asked them,

Jesus: Do you think that because these Galileans suffered in this way, they were worse sinners than all other Galileans? No, I tell you; but unless you repent, you will all perish as they did. Or those eighteen who were killed when the tower of Siloam fell on them — do you think that they were worse offenders than all the others living in Jerusalem? No, I tell you; but unless you repent, you will all perish just as they did.

Narrator: Then he told this parable: A man had a fig tree planted in his vineyard; and he came looking for fruit on it and found none. So, he said to the gardener,

Owner: See here! For three years I have come looking for fruit on this fig tree, and still I find none. Cut it down! Why should it be wasting the soil?

Narrator: He replied,

Gardener: Sir, let it alone for one more year, until I dig around it and put manure on it. If it bears fruit next year, well and good; but if not, you can cut it down.

In tough times, don't blame the victim

Luke's narrative builds up the tension around Jesus' teaching about the urgency of the moment. 'At that very time' Jesus rebukes the crowd who are failing to seize the coming day of their liberation, some of the crowd approach him with news of Pilate's slaughter of some Galileans while they were at worship. Jesus exposed their concern for the fate of these victims as a feeble and misplaced distraction from accepting accountability for their own fate if they fail to act in line with God's justice. Rather than blame the victims of Pilate's slaughter, or blaming those killed by the collapse of a tower at Siloam of a moral failure, Jesus rejects as poor theology the view that bad things only happen to bad people. Instead, he presses the urgency of the situation facing the crowd: 'If you do not repent, you will all perish in a similar way' (13:5). This is no gentle Jesus, meek and mild. Those who persistently refuse to listen and respond decisively to God's justice will suffer deadly consequences.

The practice of blaming the victim for their suffering is alive and potent in too many corporations that perpetrate injustice upon their staff. FSU members shone a light on the practice of being blamed for their suffering as the victims of unjust work practices in Australian banks:

▷ When I spoke up about an incident involving a manager, I advised NAB I hadn't done so previously due to fear, as this manager once had pinned me down in the kitchen. I was later reprimanded for raising an issue about the lack of training!

▷ During the last 16 months on Workcover, I have been victimised by former staff colleagues. My managers have ceased contact with me, and I have never been asked about my health by my former managers. In November, a psychiatrist found it would be detrimental to my health to return to CBA.

▷ In the morning we must pledge what sales we want to get and if it's not achieved by the end of the day, we are made to feel inadequate.

▷ After working for NAB for over 3 years the sales pressure and toxic culture got to me and I developed severe anxiety, where I was unable to perform my duties. Despite seeking help from higher management and HR (Human Resources), they did nothing to assist. I was forced to resign as a result.

Take a few minutes in silence to step through this reflection.

1. Imagine you are one of the above workers. Imagine how you are feeling when you recall the experience you have shared?
2. Then imagine how you feel about the way your imagined self was treated. What do you think is unjust about that situation, which has not been acknowledged?
3. What do you imagine Jesus saying to you about your imagined situation?

Now write down what you imagined Jesus saying. When all are ready, share with your group what you have written, and why.

When all have shared, what do you notice in common about how group members have imagined Jesus speaking to them as they stood in the shoes of a victim of injustice?

Now consider in silence: how may what your group imagined Jesus' saying to victims of injustice speak to you to help you take greater personal responsibility in facing a current injustice affecting your work or another aspect of your life?

Those who are able may share how Jesus' teaching connects with their personal situation.

Reflect together on what is emerging from this conversation.

A window of opportunity: realigning imagination and practice

What God desires is unambiguous: it is repentance, or, if you prefer, the realignment of our lives with God's just purposes. The parable of the fig tree emphasises the point: time is up. God will not wait forever for our needed change. This is the last chance for the people of God. Being God's people does not entitle us to do what we please. Repentance requires 'the conversion of imagination and practice that aligns one with the ways of God... In the imagery of the parable, Jesus' activity gives God's people one more year to respond to God's gracious invitation' (Carroll, 280). The claim of divine justice joins the gift of God's forgiveness with the purpose of acting towards God's liberating intent.

RASP research suggests that transforming our imagination about injustice in the Australian finance sector may begin with acknowledging colonialism's idolatry of money and its ethic of maximising profit at the expense of God's justice. Indigenous theologian Garry Deverell wrote: 'For us, spirituality is all about the most basic building blocks of life: country, kin, and the practise of a ritual storytelling that weaves past, present and future living together in a web sometimes referred to as 'the dreaming' (Deverell, 10). Importantly, the Dreaming is kept alive in First Peoples lives by ritual storytelling.

But Deverell's indigenous heritage is 'a colonial Indigeneity' (Deverell, 19), meaning his theology will never escape its European roots or imagination. The impact of contemporary capitalism on his Indigenous identity and life purpose is pervasive, further stifled by Australian's 'continuing to exercise a strange forgetting' (Deverell, 22) about the genocide at this nation's foundation. Far more than the oppressive impact of the tempered justice of capitalist ethics, the doctrine of the 'discovery' of Australia and *terra nullius* totally denies holistic justice for Indigenous Australians. What could this mean for our study of corporate Australia and the property wealth of our churches in the face of the destructive injustices perpetrated by capitalist ethics 'white-washing' of stolen land?

Indigenous Australians have something to say about endurance in the face of profound injustice and how to struggle for holistic justice. For the source of their life as Indigenous people is grounded in the land, and because country is regarded by Indigenous people 'as a religious text' (Deverell, 24), the land speaks constantly of the wholeness of their lives. *Indigenous spirituality cannot be subsumed by capitalist ethics.* First Nations live within the strictures of a colonial/capitalist economy, but their experience of the source of their humanity is not bound by its recent experiences of Australia's capitalist economy: *Indigenous identity and purpose had its life-source in the Dreaming* long before colonial powers opened the first bank at Sydney Cove. Garry Deverell asserts there is a truth to be acknowledged in his peoples' stories, which may be the foundation for both First Nations and settler peoples' 'liberation from falsehood and lies' (Deverell, 43).

You are called to personal and corporate acts of repentance by converting your imagination and practice to align with the ways of God through an engagement with

45

truth-telling and actions for justice. Imagine you and/or your congregation of settler people to be the fig tree planted in the vineyard of Indigenous country. Fruitless in achieving reconciliation, after how many years? What are the barriers to you opening your heart to greater solidarity with First Nations people? In silence, name those barriers in your heart, before Christ.

Now, Jesus has negotiated one more year for you to be fruitful and produce good fruit from a healed, reconciled and just nation. What will you commit to converting your imagination and practice to becoming fruitful in God's sight?

Consider the following truth-telling and justice initiatives – listed after Study Five – under the heading 'Practical Action Possibilities' to which you may offer your riches of energy and money:

1. University of Divinity's Indigenous Theology Fund.
2. Indigenous culture and art: Indigenous art prize
3. Indigenous literacy and community languages: the Indigenous Literacy Fund
4. Australasian Centre for Corporate Responsibility (ACCR).
5. U Ethical, ethical investor.

Members of the group report on further information they have researched from the listed truth-telling opportunities.

Reflect on any sense of call you have to be engaged with for any of these or other opportunities to flourish.

Then discuss how you may use the next 12 months to become more fruitful.

Conclude by writing the commitment you wish to make. Also, write the name of one person with whom you will share the commitment you have made.

If you are able, share with your study group.

Closing prayer

Psalm 63: 1-8

Readers: Leader (L), People (P)

L: O God, you are my God, I seek you, my soul thirsts for you;
P: my flesh faints for you, as in a dry and weary land where there is no water.
L: So I have looked upon you in the sanctuary,
P: beholding your power and glory.
L: Because your steadfast love is better than life,
P: my lips will praise you.
L: So I will bless you as long as I live;
P: I will lift up my hands and call on your name.
L: My soul is satisfied as with a rich feast,
P: and my mouth praises you with joyful lips
L: when I think of you on my bed,
P: and meditate on you in the watches of the night;
L: for you have been my help, and in the shadow of your wings I sing for joy.
P: My soul clings to you; your right hand upholds me.

STUDY FOUR

Restorative justice: healing covetousness and hard-heartedness

Background

As Luke's account of Jesus' journey towards Jerusalem unfolds, the public response to Jesus becomes more divisive. The fault lines of conflict become clearer. There is a growing company of people who have been healed of demons and various ailments, as well as those who are poor and of low status. Many are drawn to Jesus' teaching of the coming kingdom of God that will reverse the honour and status hierarchies that exclude them from full participation in society.

Chief amongst those who oppose Jesus on his journey to Jerusalem are the Pharisees. They can see religious norms that protect their honour and status in a pagan world being turned upside down by Jesus' radical and inclusive teaching about God's purposes for Israel. It seems the Pharisees' strategy at this point is to win Jesus to their viewpoint, which hangs on maintaining their religious purity by putting up strong boundaries to exclude everything that might contaminate their central purpose. So, for the third time in Luke's gospel, Jesus is a guest at dinner in a Pharisee's home. But the more they try to draw Jesus in, the more he sees their behaviour as status and honour-seeking for themselves: having a well-respected public figure grace their table, and this exposes them to a series of Jesus' withering critiques.

But at the very moment Jesus' conflict with the Pharisees is about to come to a head, he warns those who have joined his community that they will need to make a careful assessment of their own commitment. For the violence that awaits Jesus in Jerusalem will certainly fall on them too if they remain loyal to the new order of God's realm of justice.

Luke 15:1-3, 11b-32

Eight readers are needed to read this passage: Luke (the narrator), a Pharisee, a Scribe, Jesus, Son2, Father, a slave, and Son1.

Narrator: Now all the tax collectors and sinners were coming near to listen to him. And the Pharisees and the scribes were grumbling and saying,

Pharisee: This fellow welcomes sinners

Scribe: and eats with them.

Narrator: So he told them this parable: Then Jesus said,

Jesus: There was a man who had two sons. The younger of them said to his father,

Son2: Father, give me the share of the property that will belong to me.

Narrator: So he divided his property between them. A few days later, the younger son gathered all he had and travelled to a distant country, and there he squandered his property in dissolute living. When he had spent everything, a severe famine took place throughout that country, and he began to be in need. So he went and hired himself out to one of the citizens of that country, who sent him to his fields to feed the pigs. He would gladly have filled himself with the pods that the pigs were eating; and no one gave him anything. But when he came to himself he said,

Son2: How many of my father's hired hands have bread enough and to spare, but here I am dying of hunger! I will get up and go to my father, and I will say to him, 'Father, I have sinned against heaven and before you; I am no longer worthy to be called your son; treat me like one of your hired hands'.

Narrator: So he set off and went to his father. But while he was still far off, his father saw him and was filled with compassion; he ran and put his arms around him and kissed him. Then the son said to him,

Son2: Father, I have sinned against heaven and before you; I am no longer worthy to be called your son.

Narrator: But the father said to his slaves,

Father: Quickly, bring out a robe – the best one – and put it on him; put a ring on his finger and sandals on his feet. And get the fatted calf and kill it, and let us eat and celebrate; for this son of mine was dead and is alive again; he was lost and is found!

Narrator: And they began to celebrate. Now his elder son was in the field; and when he came and approached the house, he heard music and dancing. He called one of the slaves and asked what was going on. He replied,

Slave: Your brother has come, and your father has killed the fatted calf, because he has got him back safe and sound.

Narrator: Then he became angry and refused to go in. His father came out and began to plead with him. But he answered his father,

Son1: Listen! For all these years I have been working like a slave for you, and I have never disobeyed your command; yet you have never given me even a young goat so that I might celebrate with my friends. But when this son of yours came back, who has devoured your property with prostitutes, you killed the fatted calf for him!'

Narrator: Then the father said to him,

Father: Son, you are always with me, and all that is mine is yours. But we had to celebrate and rejoice, because this brother of yours was dead and has come to life; he was lost and has been found.

Covetousness: the sin against God and neighbour

Luke directs our attention to these three parables (15:3): this one is the third. Two preceding brief parables of a lost sheep (15:4-7) and a lost coin (15:8-10) reinforce Jesus' teaching that God rejoices with the community when a lost sinner is restored to the community. With tax collectors and sinners drawing close to listen, Jesus tells these two parables to demonstrate his faith in God's gracious inclusiveness and invites the Pharisees to open their hearts to God's generous embrace. Now, in this third parable, Jesus draws his critics into the story, challenging them to also 'enact the welcoming grace of God's dominion' (Carroll, 313).

First, Jesus shows how dissolute is the younger son's behaviour, claiming his inheritance and thus treating his father as if he were already dead. The son's behaviour dishonours his father and family and brings disgrace on himself. Yet before long, the younger son's planned property development activities to achieve greater status and honour have failed, and he is overwhelmed by the depth of his ruin, sin and shame. The words of his lament – 'I have sinned *against heaven* and *before you*' – echo the confession of King David when confronted by his complicity in murder (2 Samuel 12:13). A sin against another person is first of all a sin against God.

Reflect for a time in silence on how the younger son is feeling after all his plans have fallen through. If you were the younger son, how would you feel, having sinned against God, and your father? Then share your response, and any times you have experienced similar feelings in your work and other aspects of life.

Workers in the financial industry revealed how corporation boards and senior executives' pursuit of maximised profit had the effect of normalising abusive organisational behaviour through promises of personal rewards for workers at the cost of violating their ethical integrity.

▷ When I returned to work after my injury, my Regional Manager asked if I was going to meet target that quarter, I explained that I could not possibly meet my target, having had so much time off. She said that I had two months to *look for another job*.

▷ We get *put down constantly*, and Management are only interested in delivering the results they promised and making their giant bonuses. They have no concern for staff wellbeing.

▷ The constant sales pressures and target movements had always been geared towards the CBA senior management making targets. Many times, the senior area and region management were told of the staff feeling regarding targets and the toxic lies and pressure put on staff.

▷ If a banker is not adhering to compliance or risk requirements, management will sweep it under the carpet as long as this person has the sales figures, he or she will still get bonus reward.

Now reflect for a time in silence on how these workers are feeling after being pressured to maximise their employer's profit at the expense of their human dignity and integrity.

Then share your response, and any times you have experienced similar feelings in your work and other aspects of life.

What similarities can you see between your imagining of being in the younger son's shoes and the experiences of these FSU workers?

Grace: forgiveness, healing and restorative justice

The integrity and humility of the son's confession begins a movement that transforms his circumstance from hopelessness to new life. The father saw his son coming from a distance. Was the father waiting, yearning, hoping? Before the son can complete his prepared speech, he is swept up in his father's embrace. Luke describes the father's extravagant response that flows from his compassion. The son who is not 'worthy' to be called son is restored in that role, the shameful harm of the son against his father is forgiven, and the son is reinvested with the honour of being called 'son'. It is as if a relationship that was dead has been restored to life.

Reflect for a time in silence on how the younger son is feeling as he sees his father running towards him, being embraced, then being restored to equality in his father's house and welcomed with a communal feast.

Then share your response, and any times you have experienced similar feelings in your work and other aspects of life.

What might this story mean for modern-day Australia? For over 200 years, from its beginning as a British colony, Australia, along with other Western countries, has lived a reckless life, chasing economic growth without due regard to the integrity of nature. Now we are increasingly experiencing despoiling of the environment, with climate change and ecological collapse resulting in floods, bushfire, and the devastation of a rampant pandemic, while fuelling increasing inequality between rich and poor. Who is waiting, yearning, hoping for a change of heart? That voice comes as 'The Uluru Statement from the Heart'.

> Our Aboriginal and Torres Strait Islander tribes were the first sovereign Nations of the Australian continent and its adjacent islands, and possessed it under our own laws and customs. This our ancestors did, according to the reckoning of our culture, from the Creation, according to the common law from 'time immemorial', and according to science more than 60,000 years ago.
>
> *This sovereignty is a spiritual notion: the ancestral tie between the land, or 'mother nature', and the Aboriginal and Torres Strait Islander peoples who were born therefrom, remain attached thereto, and must one day return thither*

to be united with our ancestors. This link is the basis of the ownership of the soil, or better, of sovereignty.

It has never been ceded or extinguished, and co-exists with the sovereignty of the Crown. How could it be otherwise? That peoples possessed a land for sixty millennia and this sacred link disappears from world history in merely the last two hundred years?

With substantive constitutional change and structural reform, we believe this ancient sovereignty can shine through as a fuller expression of Australia's nationhood.

Proportionally, we are the most incarcerated people on the planet. We are not an innately criminal people. Our children are aliened from their families at unprecedented rates. This cannot be because we have no love for them. And our youth languish in detention in obscene numbers. They should be our hope for the future. These dimensions of our crisis tell plainly the structural nature of our problem. *This is the torment of our powerlessness.*

We seek constitutional reforms to empower our people and take a *rightful place* in our own country. When we have power over our destiny, our children will flourish. They will walk in two worlds and their culture will be a gift to their country.

We call for the establishment of a First Nations Voice enshrined in the Constitution.

Makarrata is the culmination of our agenda: *the coming together after a struggle.* It captures our aspirations for a fair and truthful relationship with the people of Australia and a better future for our children based on justice and self-determination.

We seek a Makarrata Commission to supervise a process of agreement-making between governments and First Nations and truth-telling about our history.

In 1967 we were counted, in 2017 we seek to be heard. We leave base camp and start our trek across this vast country. We invite you to walk with us in a movement of the Australian people for a better future.

Reflect for a time on what you would say to a First Nations person about the way their sovereignty has been ignored through colonial invasion of this continent. Write what you would say and share it with one other person in the study.

Then reflect for a time in silence on how a person with a settler inheritance feels receiving this *Statement from the Heart*. How do you feel as you hear the anguished truth and heart-felt compassion in these words?

Share a time of reflection with your paired partner. Be aware of the anguished truth and heart-felt compassion in the father's embrace of his prodigal son.

Then consider the level of congruence between the father's compassion and what you know of Christ's desire to restore First Nations people and settlers to full relationship in a reconciled nation.

The struggle to turn from self-justification to God's justice

Now we come to the final part of our parable. The older brother refuses his father's invitation to the feast, a refusal that puts him on a par with his brother in also dishonouring his father. The older brother accuses his father of treating him like a slave, turns his back on his younger brother and refuses to acknowledge him as kin, and rudely complains that his own hard work has never been rewarded with any celebration.

Despite his older son's repudiation of both his father's status and his brother's restoration, again the father's words carry anguish and compassion, but this time for his recalcitrant older son. The father reassures the older son that he inherits everything his father possesses. Faced by the older son's hard-heartedness, the father's grace, and intent to reconcile his sons and restore them as equal persons in his family is undiminished. While the younger son is reconciled and restored after repenting of his abuse and shaming of his father, the older son is offered reconciliation within his father's family and restored to his privileged place in his father's family without repenting of his abuse and shaming of both his father and brother. The point is that God's compassion is larger than the Pharisees' legalism understood, which insisted repentance must precede forgiveness and reconciliation. But the outcome of the parable is open-ended, resting in the older brother's hand. So, while Jesus reaches out to the Pharisees with this same unconditional grace to touch their hearts and bring them to a point of sharing God's gracious and inclusive love, Luke's narrative will reveal that the Pharisees will concede nothing. Indeed, as we will learn soon, they are willing to become complicit in murder to hold onto their status and privilege.

A number of FSU members demonstrated how their own integrity and concern revealed their greater empathy and service for their customers than their corporation's rules-based monetary rewards for maximising profit from bank customers. They were not willing to be complicit in violence against their customers to maintain their privileged position in their workplace.

▷ I am astounded by my resilience, working in such an unethical industry. Even when my manager tells me I need to be more resilient I laugh on the inside because I know *I still have the courage to face this toxic industry* every single day.

▷ I'm now fully aware of my skill set and can *hold my head high* with a personal brand of integrity.

▷ I have always served customers with integrity. CBA uses the financial health check model saying it's to help customers with all their banking needs but *it's just really another tool designed to sell* more products.

▷ If you questioned anything from middle or upper management, you became tarnished for having an opinion. I discovered it was about forcing products on people that either don't need or couldn't afford them. *I refused to do wrong by the customer just for targets.*

Reflect on what equips people such as the father in the parable and these workers to maintain their compassion for others when they are threatened by abuse and violence. Share with others in your group.

Then consider: What links the struggles for sovereignty of First Nations people to settler peoples' struggles for justice in an Australian society based on capitalist ethics of profit maximisation, which tempers justice?

Reflect together in silence for a time.

Then quickly brainstorm and record on a white-board as a group the theological, political, economic, and psychological factors that may link these struggles.

Place this list firmly before your group as you pray the closing prayer.

Closing prayer

Psalm 32

Readers: Leader (L), voice one (V1), voice two (V2), voice three (V3), all.
Selah is thought to be a musical direction and need not be spoken.

**All: Happy are those whose transgression is forgiven,
  whose sin is covered.**
**Happy are those to whom the Lord imputes no iniquity,
  and in whose spirit there is no deceit.**
V1: While I kept silence, my body wasted away
  through my groaning all day long.
V2: For day and night your hand was heavy upon me;
  my strength was dried up as by the heat of summer.
  Selah

V1: Then I acknowledged my sin to you,
  and I did not hide my iniquity;
V2: I said, 'I will confess my transgressions to the Lord',
  and you forgave the guilt of my sin.
  Selah

L: Therefore let all who are faithful offer prayer to you;
at a time of distress, the rush of mighty waters shall not
reach them.
V1: You are a hiding-place for me; you preserve me from
trouble;
  you surround me with glad cries of deliverance.
  Selah

V3: I will instruct you and teach you the way you should go;
   I will counsel you with my eye upon you.
Do not be like a horse or a mule, without understanding,
   whose temper must be curbed with bit and bridle,
   else it will not stay near you.

All: Many are the torments of the wicked,
but steadfast love surrounds those who trust in the Lord.
Be glad in the Lord and rejoice, O righteous,
and shout for joy, all you upright in heart.

STUDY FIVE

Love and solidarity within the shadow of death

Background

In John's Gospel, our journey with Jesus brings us to the outskirts of Jerusalem and the village of Bethany, where Lazarus had been ill and has died. John's narrative seeks to help us better understand what Jesus' death and resurrection means for our faith in the God who brings life out of death. Lazarus' death is real, a consequence of his illness, just as Jesus' death will be real and is a consequence of the coalition of forces that decide Jesus must die to protect their own status and privilege. John is inviting us to 'come and see' (11:34) that God is present amid the world's injustice, violence, tears and grief. Yet even as Lazarus is raised to life from death, we are asked to prepare for Jesus' journey *through* death into a new sort of life.

John's hard-headed realism insists that we understand the painful death Jesus will endure is a consequence of the ultimate betrayal of religious 'freedom' by the religious establishment. The chief priests' fear that any whiff of a Jewish uprising would bring down the full force of Roman law and order on Jerusalem had convinced them that Jesus' proximity to their capital was a real threat. They feared Jesus' presence had the potential to lead an uprising against their Jewish religio/political order that would destabilise their *quid pro quo* with the Romans, and therefore had to be shut down quickly. The establishment's need to maintain the status quo free of Roman interference led to their calculated decision to give the order to have Jesus arrested. The shadow of Jesus' death hangs over the next scene.

John 12:1-8

Three readers are needed to read this passage: John (the narrator), Judas and Jesus.

Narrator: Six days before the Passover Jesus came to Bethany, the home of Lazarus, whom he had raised from the dead. There they gave a dinner for him. Martha served, and Lazarus was one of those at the table with him. Mary took a pound of costly perfume made of pure nard, anointed Jesus' feet, and wiped them with her hair. The house was filled with the fragrance of the perfume. But Judas Iscariot, one of his disciples (the one who was about to betray him), said,

Judas: Why was this perfume not sold for three hundred denarii and the money given to the poor?

Narrator: (He said this not because he cared about the poor, but because he was a thief; he kept the common purse and used to steal what was put into it.) Jesus said,

Jesus: Leave her alone. She bought it so that she might keep it for the day of my burial. You always have the poor with you, but you do not always have me.'

The whisper of death

The allusion to his death is explicit in Jesus' grim reminder that 'you do not always have me'. But John knows that the shadow of death is already present in the malevolent presence of the betrayer before Jesus spoke these words. Judas knows the importance of good public relations to disguise his deadly self-aggrandising scheme. His sham concern for 'the poor' will soon serve as his cover (13:29) when he later leaves their Passover meal to betray Jesus to the authorities. If Judas' intent with his outburst was to distract the disciples from the threat of Jesus' impending death, Jesus was having none of it. Jesus' response shows that he knows full well the reality before him, and hence his appreciation of Mary's solidarity with him. Her anointing of Jesus prior to the terrible death that awaits him is in stark contrast to those who fear he has undermined their collusion with Roman power, causing them to see Jesus as a threat of whom they are best rid.

RASP research into the work experiences of 353 FSU members reported to the union during the 2018 Royal Commission into Banking identified ten cases of attempted suicide and suicidal thinking. In one case after another, there is a managerial voice akin to that of Judas that seeks to deflect attention from the threat to one person of death's shadow due to malignant forces in the workplace by pointing to the supposedly more important needs of the corporation, such as:

▷ After 12 months, constant pressure and failed discussions with management, I attempted to take my own life.

I consulted a doctor, whereby they referred me to a psychologist who diagnosed me with PTSD and advised to go on Workcover. I told my manager this, who advised that *it would affect the business*. I remain on Workcover even until this day.

▷ For 2 years, I was picked on by management. I tried to commit suicide and had to attend Royal Perth Hospital. In the end, due to depression, they terminated my contract through ill health, *something that their own Doctor did not recommend*.

▷ The amount of pressure to produce results and sales led me to holding a knife against my wrist and nearly committing suicide. My manager had led me to feel like I wanted to commit suicide and you know what their response was? 'We find that *your allegation of bullying and harassment is unsubstantiated* and this matter has been resolved.' I was like, 'how can this be true?' This all happened.

▷ We are threatened and bullied. They promise to change and get rid of targets. However, in the case of the CBA they only change the name. My husband came home one night while I was thinking of driving to the beach and just walking into the ocean. They are not human and *don't consider the effect of their attitude* on staff and customers.

Imagine you are one of these bank workers contemplating suicide to escape from soul-destroying work pressure and personal denigration by your boss. How do you feel about your work? How do you feel recalling the deflecting and minimising comments of your boss as you remember attempting to end your life?

Share your reflection with the group.

Then consider: the Australian Institute of Health and Welfare reported 'the rate for suicide of Indigenous Australians is almost twice the rate of all non-Indigenous Australians (24.6 per 100,000 and 12.5 per 100,000, respectively). Suicide was... the leading cause of death for Indigenous children aged 5–17 years' ('Indigenous mental health and suicide prevention', 2019). Reported causes are rooted in generational trauma from colonial violation of that which gives life: country, kin, dreaming.

What links the struggles for community mental health and justice of First Nations people to settler peoples' struggles to escape from soul-destroying work pressure and personal denigration in workplaces driven by the capitalist ethics of profit maximisation? What links these struggles, and what are the critical differences?

Reflect on your experience of how death in general, and suicide in particular, have been responded to in workplaces or communities that you have experienced. What is it like when someone has an attitude like Judas to First Nations and/or settler people's injustice and suffering: they attempt to minimise other people's pain and grief, and deflect the conversation away by pushing to 'move on' with something they say is more important?

Share your reflection with the group.

The value of life

Instead of holding a wake for Lazarus' death, thanks to Jesus' prayerful intervention, this intimate group of brother and sisters is able to gather with Jesus and his disciples for a celebration dinner for Lazarus' life. This dinner serves to look back to Lazarus' death and his restoration to life, and also looks forward to Jesus' impending confrontation with the deadly forces arraigned in opposition to him. Mary grasps the terrible truth at the heart of this crisis point in Jesus' journey towards Jerusalem with her extravagant anointing of Jesus' feet, and the profoundly intimate gesture of wiping his feet with her hair. She understands that death's shadow is approaching her friend and Lord, and her love for him is poured out in a beautiful symbolic action. The dark reality of death is transformed by the unconditional love expressed between Mary and Jesus as its holy, fragrant presence fills the space in which they are gathered.

Consider the following excerpt from a RASP article on suicide prevention, where the value of life emerges from the shadow of death.

> The workers' stories reclaim the vulnerability of being both dependent on others for support and interdependent with others for a deeper sense of self and self-worth. Through the mutuality of their participation in the FSU project to address the Royal Commission, each worker re-asserted their interdependent self, that is, each storied submission to the FSU portal 'stands for a moment of life in which one can feel committed to service, willing to become anybody for others' (Kim, 2013).

> The workers' stories challenge the alienation and powerlessness caused by management's discrediting definitions of the worker's self-worth, by affirming workers' humanity when they are vulnerable. While they give voice to feelings of weakness, betrayal and injustice, their narratives demonstrate strength and purpose in offering the wholeness of their experience of vulnerability. Their stories demonstrate courage in pushing back against the injustice they experienced through management's unjust treatment (Flett, et al. unpublished).

Imagine again that you are one of these bank workers contemplating suicide to escape from soul-destroying work pressure devoted to maximising profit and personal denigration by your boss. Imagine Mary coming to you and comforting you with her generous love and tenderness for your pain and fear. How do you feel? What touched you about her solidarity with you?

Share your reflection with the group.

What is it about Mary's relationship with Jesus that you might wish for yourself in living out what is of ultimate value for you in your use of money and/or what is precious in your life?

Share your reflection with the group.

How might this study group support you to live a story of generous love and tenderness in sharing your gifts for those:

a. who have suffered the bitterness of betrayal and mistreatment in their work or other aspects of their life, and/or,

b. who are suffering the intergenerational trauma of colonialism's economic, political, and religious violence?

Share your reflection with the group.

What would you like to report to:

a. Your church council about what direction/action your study group plans to take in future?
b. The Religion and Social Policy Network of the University of Divinity about what direction/action your study group/congregation plans to take in future?

Please forward your response to:

Rev'd Dr Richard Wilson
Secretary
Religion and Social Policy Network
University of Divinity
90 Albion Road,
Box Hill Vic. 3128

Closing prayer

Psalm 126

Readers: Leader (L), People (P)

L: When the Lord restored the fortunes of Zion,
P: we were like those who dream.
L: Then our mouth was filled with laughter,
P: and our tongue with shouts of joy;
L: then it was said among the nations,
P: 'The Lord has done great things for them'.
L: The Lord has done great things for us,
P: and we rejoiced.
L: Restore our fortunes, O Lord,
P: like the watercourses in the Negeb.
L: May those who sow in tears
P: reap with shouts of joy.
L: Those who go out weeping, bearing the seed for sowing,
All: shall come home with shouts of joy, carrying their sheaves.

PRACTICAL ACTION POSSIBILITIES

Truth-telling

Indigenous Theology Fund

The University of Divinity is committed to encouraging the development of Aboriginal and Torres Strait Islander theologies and ministries, through its School of Indigenous Studies and related activities. Donations to the University's Indigenous Theology Fund support Indigenous people to study, research, teach, and provide academic and pastoral support.

Donations of $2 or more are allowable deductions for income tax purposes in Australia.

https://divinity.edu.au/giving/

Indigenous culture and art

Wiradjuri man Glenn Loughrey's art is an expression of the journey of his family and mob. It reflects the interaction between the dominant culture and the oldest living culture on the planet. It explores the impact of that interaction from the Indigenous point of view and its purpose is to engage, challenge and initiate action leading to unification and reconciliation. Each of Glenn's paintings invites the viewer to touch and engage beyond simply being a viewer or observer. His art is political because Glenn believes all of life is political if lived consciously or mindfully, or as he understands Aboriginal thinking, with deep listening (whin-nga-rra) to the country or the dirt that gave you birth. Glenn has earmarked all contributions for truth telling through art for the development of an art prize/scholarship/ commission project for emerging indigenous creatives. Funding required for this project is $5,000. All donations to the project will receive a tax-deductible receipt, and donors will be invited to the opening exhibition.

Find out more of Glenn's art at:
https://glennloughrey.com/about

Please forward your contribution to this exciting and timely project at St Oswald's Aboriginal Creative Fund.
https://www.melbourneanglican.org.au/maf-donation-page/

Indigenous literacy and community languages
The Indigenous Literacy Foundation supports Indigenous literacy and development of community languages by providing new, culturally appropriate books to communities that need them; promoting early literacy and familiarity with books in children under five, with a dedicated story-time session; supporting carers to share books with their children in home languages and in English; and producing and publishing books by Indigenous people for Indigenous people. These books are important because they represent culture, community life and language.

Details of the Foundation:
https://www.indigenousliteracyfoundation.org.au/
A donation to the work of the Foundation may be made at:
www.ilf.org.au/donate

Investor justice projects

Australasian Centre for Corporate Responsibility (ACCR)

ACCR is a research and shareholder advocacy organisation. Their focus is on how listed Australian companies, industry associations and investors are managing climate, labour, human rights and governance issues. ACCR holds a small portfolio of shares for the purpose of engaging with companies, including through the filing of shareholder resolutions.

They are philanthropically funded, not-for-profit and in-dependent. ACCR relies on grants and donations to fund their work, engaging the investment sector to improve corporate behaviour and transparency on Environmental, Social and Governance issues.

You can support ACCR to utilise shareholder resolutions and other mechanisms to hold ASX listed companies to account on issues by making a non-taxable donation to ACCR, or making a tax-deductible donation to ACCR's research fund, which has Deductible Gift Recipient (DGR) status.

Call 02 7251 6767 or email us at office@accr.org.au and we will get in touch with you and discuss the best way to proceed.

U Ethical

U Ethical is an ethical investment manager investing for the purpose of making a better world and a not-for-profit social enterprise of the Uniting Church in Australia. U Ethical advocates for investors' environmental and social concerns about corporate behaviour by holding companies to account.

You can support U Ethical's commitment to restore social mutuality and bring benefit to a broader range of stakeholders by signing up to an emerging network of individual and church investors. You can contribute by:

- Letter writing and personal representations to your local Member of Parliament or ministers about strengthening social and environmental justice in Federal legislation for the financial services industry.
- Contacting your bank about your concerns with its social, environmental and governance practices and policies.
- Volunteering to coordinate campaigns with like-minded church members to bring about needed change in the finance sector.

When you join this network, you will be given access to U Ethical's up-to-date intelligence on opportunities for engagement with justice initiatives for ethically driven social and environmental change research, and links to other ethical investor activists with informed strategies for environmental, social and good governance practices.

Register to join the ethical investor network and indicate your areas of interest by emailing the Ethics and Impact unit Desiree.Lucchese@uethical.com and learn how to maximise the impact of your personal and/or church's investments for the common good.

BIBLIOGRAPHY

Australian Institute of Health and Welfare, *Indigenous mental health and suicide prevention*, Canberra, 2019.

Carroll, J. T., *Luke: a commentary*, Westminster John Knox Press, Louisville Kentucky: 2012.

Ci, Jiwei, 'Justice, Freedom, and the Moral Bounds of Capitalism', *Social Theory and Practice*, 25/3,1999. pp. 409-438.

Deverell, G. W., *Gondwana Theology: a Trawloolway man reflects on Christian Faith*. Reservoir: Morning Star Publishing, 2018.

Ferguson, A., *Banking Bad: Whistleblowers. Corporate cover-ups. One journalist's fight for the truth*, Australia: Harper Collins Publishers, 2019.

Flett, J., Byrne, B., and Bottomley, J., *Justice Tempered: how the finance sector's captivity to capitalist ethics violates workers' ethical integrity and silences their claims for justice*. Melbourne, Religion and Social Policy Network, University of Divinity, 2020.

_____ , *'I held a knife against my wrist'*: ethical conflict and work harm in Australian Financial Services. Melbourne,

Religion and Social Policy Network, University of Divinity, 2020.

_____ , *Suicide Prevention in Australian Financial Services: Work-Related Suicide in Political, Cultural and Ethical Context* (Unpublished, 2021).

JusticeFSU-final-report.draft_.pdf (fsunion.org.au).

Portal_study_final.pdf (netdna-ssl.com).

Report of the Royal Commission into Misconduct in the Banking, Superannuation and Financial Services Industry. Interim Report, 2018, vol.1.

The Uluru Statement from the Heart, 2017 National Constitution Convention,

The Statement — https://ulurustatement.org/the-statement (accessed 19/10/2021).